JAZZ CLARINET STUDIES

James Rae

CONTENTS

© 1993 by Faber Music Ltd
This edition published in 2006 by Faber Music Ltd
Music processed by Donald Sheppard
Cover illustration by Vikki Liogier
Printed in England by Caligraving Ltd
All rights reserved

ISBN 0-571-52646-2

To buy Faber Music publications or to find out about the full range of titles available
please contact your local music retailer or Faber Music sales enquiries:

Faber Music Limited, Burnt Mill, Elizabeth Way, Harlow, CM20 2HX England
Tel: +44 (0)1279 82 89 82   Fax: +44 (0)1279 82 89 83
sales@fabermusic.com   fabermusic.com

Introduction

This book is designed to assist classically trained musicians with the interpretation of jazz music. Comparing the interpretation of jazz music to that of classical can be likened to the comparison between spoken American and spoken English. They are both written in more or less the same way but sound totally different. The best way to acquire a strong American accent is to live there for a while – the sound of the language is absorbed and it becomes natural to adopt the same dialect. With jazz, it is also essential to listen carefully to players in this idiom in order to develop a 'feel' for jazz in your own playing.

Using the book

The aim in part I is for the student to absorb the essential rhythmic devices of jazz music. It begins with the concept of swing rhythm, and then works through various types of anticipated beat and syncopation.

Part 2 contains melodious jazz studies, arranged progressively. These incorporate, in various combinations, the rhythms established in Part I.

In Part 3 the studies are of a more technical nature allowing the student to absorb many of the tonalities used in jazz.

Important note for examination candidates

This book was originally published in two volumes: *Progressive Jazz Studies* – Easy and Intermediate level. ABRSM and Trinity Guildhall examination candidates should therefore note the following changes of numbering of the later studies:

Previous study number	New study number
44	30
45	31
46	32
57	43
58	44
60	46
61	47
62	48
63	49

1. ASPECTS OF JAZZ RHYTHM

Rhythm is arguably the most important element in jazz music, and a good sense of
rhythm is one of the jazz musician's most valuable assets.

Swing quavers

Lengthen the first and shorten the second of each pair of notes.

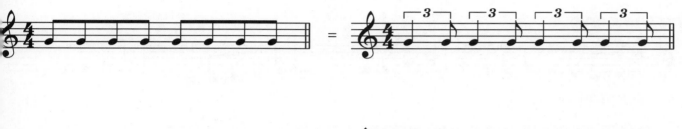

- Try clapping the rhythm before playing.
- Always use soft-tonguing where no slurs or accents are marked.

N.B.

All quavers in jazz (unless in a rock or latin context, or otherwise indicated) are
played in swing time.

4

Anticipation

Bringing forward the main beats in the bar by a quaver.

Anticipated 1st beat

It is stylistically correct to accent off-beats in jazz music.

6

Anticipated 2nd beat

Anticipated 3rd beat

Anticipated 4th beat

Syncopation

Off-beat crotchets

* Off-beat crotchets are generally played short in jazz music.

2. MELODIC JAZZ STUDIES

11

3. STUDIES IN VARIOUS TONALITIES

The blues scale

The blues scale is one of the most common features of jazz.

The blues scale in C

Familiarize yourself with this scale, and learn to play (and sing) it in every key. Then play the following studies.

The whole-tone scale and augmented arpeggio (chord)

The whole-tone scale is made up entirely of whole-tone intervals:

Because these are all equal intervals, there are only two versions of the scale
before duplication takes place:

○ = augmented chord/arpeggio

The whole-tone scale is related to the augmented chord/arpeggio. It can be used
when the symbol + or aug. appears after the chord symbol, e.g. G+ or G aug.

The following studies demonstrate this scale and chord/arpeggio in practice.

The diminished scale and arpeggio (chord)

The diminished scale is made up of alternate tones and semitones:

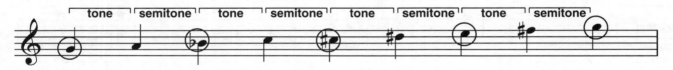

○ = diminished chord/arpeggio

Made up of a regular pattern of intervals, there are only three different versions of
the **diminished scale** before duplication takes place. For example, the scale on G
will contain the same notes as those on B♭, C♯ and E. This quality is also shared
by the diminished chord/arpeggio.

The following are studies based on all three diminished scales and arpeggios.

Modes

Often used by jazz musicians, modes can be described as scales beginning on different degrees of the major scale. There are seven basic modes:

1. The Ionian mode (the major scale)

Accompanying chord
C(maj7)

2. The Dorian mode (on the 2nd)

Dm7

3. The Phrygian mode (on the 3rd)

Em7

4. The Lydian mode (on the 4th)

F(maj7)

5. The Mixolydian mode (on the 5th)

G7

6. The Aeolian mode (on the 6th)

Am7

7. The Locrian mode (on the 7th)

half diminished
BØ

The Ionian, Dorian and Mixolydian are the most commonly used modes in jazz.
When you are familiar with the different character of each of the modes go on
to the mode studies.

Dorian mode studies

Mixolydian mode studies

The II – V7 – I Sequence

Chord II, followed by chord V7 followed by chord I (e.g. in C major, Dm7 G7 C) is probably the most common chord progression in jazz music. The following five studies are designed to familiarize the student with this progression in all the major keys. As the studies follow the same chord sequence and structure they can all be played simultaneously.